Student Workbook to accompany
INSTRUMENTAL ARRANGING

Student Workbook to accompany
INSTRUMENTAL ARRANGING

GARY WHITE
Iowa State University

Boston, Massachusetts   Burr Ridge, Illinois   Dubuque, Iowa
Madison, Wisconsin   New York, New York   San Francisco, California   St. Louis, Missouri

McGraw-Hill

A Division of The McGraw-Hill Companies

Contents

To the student:

The workbook to accompany *Instrumental Arranging* includes exercises of several kinds:

1.   Questions and problems that test your knowledge of the factual materials presented in the chapters. These are usually objective questions which have only one correct answer. Their purpose is to help you learn the many pieces of information that you must have at your fingertips as you develop skill as an arranger.

2.   Ear-training exercises that test your ability to hear various instruments and instrumental combinations. Some of these problems are very easy, but others are much more subtle and will require repeated listening to identify the instruments playing. You should not expect to hear every instrument in thick textures, and you may need to make some educated guesses in such cases. As an arranger, you must have a thorough awareness of the unique tonal characteristics of each instrument/voice in each of its registers and the sound of various instrumental combinations. The assignments will help you develop this skill, but they are only a beginning. You should make careful listening to the sounds of the various instruments a part of your daily experience.

3.   Transcription assignments that give you the opportunity to develop skill as an orchestrator. Your answers to these problems will likely differ from those of fellow students, and there is no single correct answer. Performance, either in or outside of class will help you to judge the effectiveness of your scoring.

4.   Creative assignments that encourage you to use your own musical imagination. These projects are purposefully open ended, and there is no single "correct" answer. Your instructor may substitute different projects, or you may wish to exercise your own creative ability by suggesting alternatives to the given assignments.

Many of the musical examples in this book are recorded on the compact disks that are available from the publisher. This set of CDs are specially mastered to allow you instantaneous access to the examples, and the specific disk and track number is noted for each exercise. Constant listening is critical for developing skill as an arranger, and these compact disks will make your task much easier.

I would like to recognize the valuable contributions of the following persons and groups who have helped to shape the workbook to accompany *Instrumental Arranging*: Roger Bissell, trombonist and arranger at Disneyland, wrote the assignments for chapter 19. Prof. Roger Cichy, director of Iowa State University Marching Band, wrote the assignments for chapter 20. Janice Coleman, my student assistant throughout the project, developed some of the assignment materials and did the research for others. Sara Compton, my longtime assistant, produced most of the musical examples. Prof. Anthony Lis and the students at South Dakota State University class tested the earliest version of the book. Prof. Milan Kaderavek and the students at Drake University class tested later versions. My own students at Iowa State University were also involved in class testing and found many errors and inconsistencies. The comments and critiques by students have been my most valuable resource in perfecting these materials, and I am greatly in their debt.

1   <u>Music Notation and Transposition</u>

A.   Practice making elliptical noteheads on the staves provided below. In the treble clef draw a C major scale in quarter notes, half notes, and whole notes. In the bass clef make notes in various registers, particularly emphasizing notes in ledger lines above and below the staff. (Be careful of stem direction for quarter and half notes.) Try to make the noteheads as similar to the printed symbols as possible.

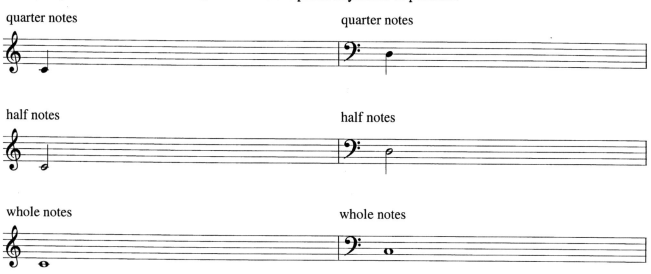

B.   Practice drawing each of the rests indicated below. Try to make your rests look similar to the printed symbols (but shading is not necessary if you are using a pencil).

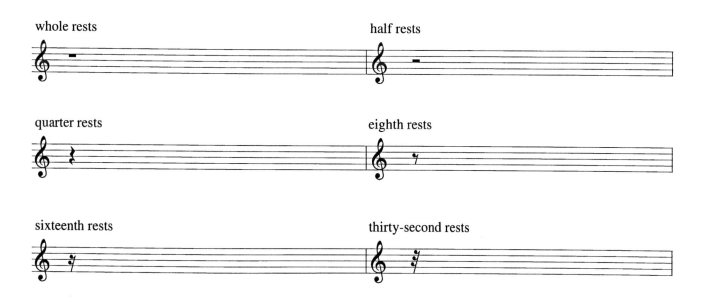

C.   Draw the notes and rests indicated.

1.   A full measure of quarter notes followed by a full measure of rest in the following meters: $\frac{3}{4}$, $\frac{4}{4}$, $\frac{6}{4}$.

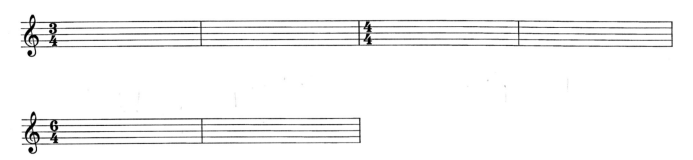

2.   A full measure of eighth notes followed by a full measure of rest in the following meters: $\frac{6}{8}$, $\frac{3}{8}$, $\frac{5}{8}$.

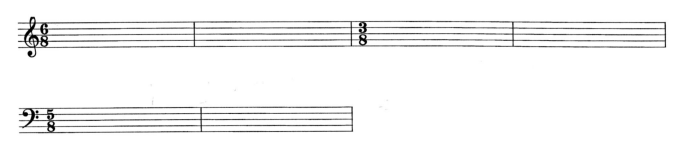

D.   Add stems to the noteheads in the following melodies. Make sure the stems are the proper length, go in the right direction, and are on the correct side of the notehead. Refer to the text if you are in doubt.

L.   Complete the following:

     1.   In instrumental music, dynamic markings appear _____ the staff.

     2.   In vocal music, dynamic markings appear _____ the staff.

     3.   When two parts are written on one staff, if the dynamics for the upper part differ

              from those of the lower part, they are written _____ the staff.

M.   Complete the following transposition exercises:

     1.   Transpose this melody down from the key of D major to the key of B-flat major.

Weber: Oberon Overture.

2. Transpose this melody up from the key of D major to the key of F major.

Weber: Oberon Overture.

3. Transpose this example down from the key of A major to the key of D major.

Weber: Oberon Overture.

Adagio sostenuto

4. Transpose this melody up from the key of D major to the key of E major.

Weber: Oberon Overture.

5. Transpose the following melody down from the key of E-flat major to the key of B-flat major.

Wagner: Overture to *Lohengrin.*

Langsam und feierlich

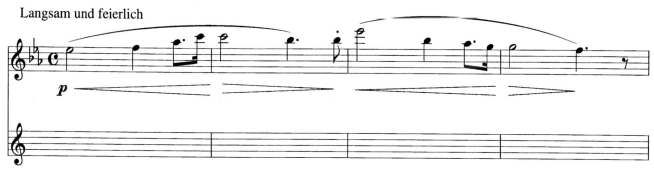

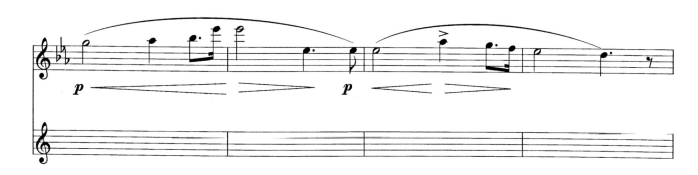

6.   Transpose this melody up from the key of C major to the key of D-flat major.

Wagner: Overture to *Die Meistersinger von Nürnberg.*

7.   Transpose the following example down from the key of F major to the key of E-flat major.

Wagner: Overture to *Lohengrin.*

8.   Transpose this melody up from the key of A-flat major to the key of D-flat major.

Tchaikovsky: Overture to *Romeo et Juliette.*

9.   Transpose the following melody up from the key of B-flat major to the key of G major.

Tchaikovsky: Fifth Symphony, 1st movement.

10.   Transpose the following line up from the key of D major to the key of E major.

Tchaikovsky: Nutcracker Suite, op. 71a, III *(Valse des Fleurs.)*

11.   Transpose this melody up from the key of D major to the key of B major.

Tchaikovsky: Romeo and Juliette Overture.

12.   Transpose the following example down from the key of C major to the key of A major.

Tchaikovsky: Symphony no. 5 in E Minor, op. 64, I (Allegro.)

2   Preparation of Scores and Parts

A.   Arrange the following lists of instruments in standard score order on the blanks to the right of each list. There may be more than one acceptable arrangement.

    1.   Woodwind instruments (concert band order):

Alto Clarinet	1._____
Alto Flute	2._____
Alto Saxophone	3._____
Baritone Saxophone	4._____
Bass Clarinet	5._____
Bassoon	6._____
B-flat Clarinet	7._____
Contrabass Clarinet	8._____
Contrabassoon	9._____
E-flat Clarinet	10._____
English Horn	11._____
Flute	12._____
Oboe	13._____
Tenor Saxophone	14._____

    2.   Brass instruments (concert band order):

Euphonium	1._____
Horn	2._____
Trombone	3._____
Trumpet	4._____
Tuba	5._____

3.   Percussion and additional instruments (orchestral order):

Chorus   1._____

Harp   2._____

Percussion   3._____

Piano   4._____

Soloist(s)   5._____

Timpani   6._____

4.   String instruments:

Bass   1._____

'Cello   2._____

Viola   3._____

Violin   4._____

B.   The following excerpts are written for a variety of instruments. (You may need to consult appendix C of the text for foreign names of instruments.)

1.   This excerpt from the Mozart clarinet concerto (K. 622) is written for an orchestra including the following instruments:

Bass (Contrabasso)

Two Bassoons (Fagotti)

'Cello (Violoncello)

Two Flutes (Flauti)

Two Horns in A (Corni in A)

Solo Clarinet in A (Clarinetto principale in A)

Viola (Viola)

Violin I (Violino I)

Violin II (Violino II)

The pairs of woodwind and brass instruments are written on single staves.

Place the instrument labels on the score in the proper places. (The key signatures, clefs, and bar lines may assist you in finding the proper label for each line. Consult appendix A in the text for the standard clefs for each instrument.)

Mozart: *Konzert für Klarinette,* K. 622.

Fundamentals

Name_____

Date_____

2.   Extract parts for each of the following instruments from the Mozart clarinet concerto excerpt above:

    a.   Flute I

b.   Bassoon II

c. Horn I

Name

Date

d.   Viola

e.   Bass

3.   The following excerpt from Darius Mihaud's *Suite Française* is written for a concert band with the following instrumentation:

Baritone (Euphonium)

Bassoons I-II (one staff)

B-flat Bass Clarinet

B-flat Bass Saxophone

B-flat Clarinets I-II-III

B-flat Cornets I-II-III (II-III on one staff)

B-flat Tenor Saxophone

B-flat Trumpets I-II (one staff)

E-flat Alto Clarinet

E-flat Alto Saxophones I-II (one staff)

E-flat Baritone Saxophone

E-flat Clarinet

Flutes I-II (one staff)

Horns in F I-II-III-IV (I-II on one staff, III-IV on one staff)

Oboes I-II (one staff)

Piccolo

Snare Drum and Cymbals

String Bass

Timpani

Trombones I-II-III (I-II on one staff)

Tubas

Place the instrument labels in the proper places on the score. (Notice that this score has no key signatures, but is a transposed score.)

Milhaud: *Suite Française,* 1. Normandie, m. 1-5.

4.   Aaron Copland's "Walk to the Bunkhouse" from The Red Pony has been scored for a concert band with the following instrumentation:

Bassoons I-II (one staff)

B-flat Bass Clarinet

B-flat Clarinets I-II

B-flat Contrabass Clarinet

B-flat Cornets I-II-III (II-III on one staff)

B-flat Tenor Saxophone

B-flat Trumpets I-II (one staff)

E-flat Alto Saxophones I-II (one staff)

E-flat Baritone Saxophone

Flutes I-II (one staff)

Horns in F I-II-III (I-II on one staff)

Oboes I-II (one staff)

Piano

Piccolo

String Bass

Trombones I-II-III-IV (I-II on one staff, III-IV on one staff)

Place the instrument labels in the proper places on this transposed score. (Some instruments are not in their usual position.)

Copland: The Red Pony, II ("Walk to the Bunkhouse")

5.   The intermezzo from Karelia Suite by Jean Sibelius is scored for an orchestra with the following instrumentation:

Bass

Bassoon I-II (on one staff)

Clarinet I-II in B-flat (on one staff)

Cymbals and Bass Drum (on one staff)

Flute I-II (on one staff)

Horns in F I-II-III-IV (I-II on one staff, III-IV on one staff)

Oboe I-II (on one staff)

Tambourine

Timpani

Trombone I-II-III-Tuba (I-II on one staff, III-Tuba on one staff)

Trumpets in F I-II-III (I-II on one staff)

Viola

Violins I-II

Violoncello

Place the instrument labels in the proper places on this score.

Sibelius: Karelia Suite, op. 11, I (Intermezzo.)

6.   The ballade from Karelia Suite by Jean Sibelius is scored for an orchestra with the following instrumentation:

Bass

Bassoon I-II (on one staff)

Clarinet I-II in A (on one staff)

English Horn

Oboe I-II (on one staff)

Viola

Violins I-II

Violoncello

Place the instrument labels in the proper places on this score.

Sibelius: Karelia Suite, op. 11, II (Ballade.)

7.   The alla marcia from Karelia Suite by Jean Sibelius is scored for an orchestra with the following instrumentation:

Bass

Bassoon I-II (on one staff)

Clarinet I-II in A (on one staff)

Cymbals and Bass Drum (on one staff)

Flute I-II (on one staff)

Horn in E I-II-III-IV (I-II on one staff, III-IV on one staff)

Oboe I-II

Piccolo

Timpani

Triangle

Trombone I-II-III-Tuba (I-II on one staff, III-Tuba on one staff)

Trumpet in F I-II-III (I-II on one staff)

Viola

Violins I-II

Violoncello

Place the instrument labels in the proper places on this score. (You will have to guess about the order of some of the percussion instruments, but make logical assignments.)

Sibelius: Karelia Suite, op. 11, III (Alla marcia.)

8.   The prelude to Wagner's Tristan and Isolde is scored for an orchestra with the following instrumentation:

Basstuba

Bassklarinette in A

Bratschen

Englisch Horn

Three Fagotte (on one staff)

Three grosse Flöten (on one staff)

Harfe

Two Hoboen

F Hörner (I-II in F on one staff, III-IV in E on one staff)

Two Klarinetten in A (on one staff)

Kontrabässe

Pauken

Three Posaunen

Three Trompeten in F (on one staff)

Violinen I-II

Violoncelle

Place the instrument labels in the proper places on this score. You will probably need to look up the German names for instruments in appendix C of the text.

Wagner: prelude to Tristan and Isolde

Langsam und schmachtend
Lento e languente

9.   Rimsky-Korsakov's Scheherazade is scored for an orchestra with the following instrumentation:

Arpa

Two Clarinetti in A (on one staff)

Contrabassi

Four Corni in F

Two Fagotti (on one staff)

Two Flauti (on one staff)

Flauto piccolo

Two Oboi (on one staff)

Timpani

Two Trombe in A (on one staff)

Three Tromboni e Tuba (I-II on one staff, III-Tuba on one staff)

Viole

Violini I

Violini II

Violoncelli

Place the instrument labels in the proper places on this score. You may need to use appendix C in the text to look up some Italian names for instruments.

Rimsky-Korsakov: Scheherazade

C.   Set up the first page of score for the following ensembles. Observe proper score order and be careful to draw the proper brackets, braces, and clefs. Refer to the text if you are in doubt.

1.   A woodwind quintet with the following instrumentation:

Bassoon, B-flat Clarinet, Flute, Horn, Oboe

2.   An ensemble with the following instrumentation:

B-Flat Clarinet, Bass, Bassoon, 'Cello, English Horn, Harp, Horn, Oboe

3.   An ensemble with the following instrumentation:

Bass, Bassoon, B-flat Clarinet, B-flat Cornet, Percussion, Trombone, Violin

4.   A brass quintet with the following instrumentation:

Horn, Trombone, Two Trumpets, Tuba

5. An ensemble consisting of Bass, 'Cello, Chorus (soprano, alto, tenor, and bass), Harp, Viola, Violin I-II:

Fundamentals

3   **An Arranger's Introduction to Musical Textures**

A.   Identify the texture types for the following short examples. Identify each texture by name (monophonic, polyphonic, homophonic, or homorhythmic). Label the elements of each texture using the following labels: PM, SM, PSM, SS, RS, HS, HRS (see page 37 in the text). Discuss your answers with classmates. Your answers may differ from those of other students. Defend your answers and listen to their explanation of their answers. There may be more than one good answer to these exercises.

1. Wagner: *Tannhäuser* Overture, m. 1–4.

2. MacDowell: Woodland Sketches, op. 51, I ("To A Wild Rose"), m. 1–8.

3. Bach: Suite no. 5 in C Minor, BWV 101, *Gigue,* m. 1-15.

4. Bach: Partita no. 2 in C Minor, BWV 826, *Rondeau,* m. 17-21.

5. Schumann: Piano Sonata, op. 11, I *(Un poco Adagio),* m. 1–5.

6. Liszt: Sonata in B Minor for piano, m. 676–679.

7. Chopin: *Tarentelle,* op. 43, m. 4–12.

8. Bach: Partita no. 6 in E Minor, BWV 830, *Gavotta,* m. 1–3.

9. Haydn: Piano Sonata in G Major, Hob. 27, I (Allegro), m. 1–28.

10. Grieg: Peer Gynt Suite, no. 2, op. 55, m. 1–10.

Name_____

Date_____

11. Mozart: String Quartet in C Major, K. 465, 1st movement, m. 1–5.

12. Chopin: Prelude no. 6, op. 28, m. 1–4.

13. Chopin: Nocturne in G Major, op. 37, no. 2, m. 1–4.

14. Chopin: Etude in A Minor, op. 25, no. 11, m. 1–6.

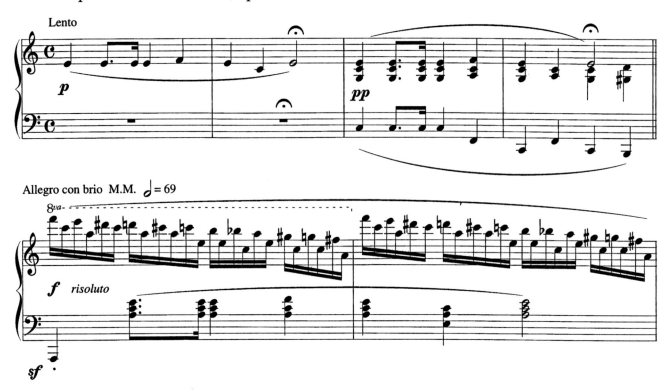

B.   Listen to each of the following excerpts on the accompanying CDs. Identify texture types and analyze the textural elements using the procedures in A above.

1. Holst: First Suite in E-flat, op. 28, no. 1, I (Chaconne), m. 1–8. (CD 3, Cut 1)

2. Holst: First Suite in E-flat, op. 28, no. 1, I (Chaconne), m. 64–69. (CD 3, Cut 4)

3. Holst: First Suite in E-flat, op. 28, no. 1, II (Intermezzo), m. 1–9. (CD 3, Cut 6)

4. Tchaikovsky: Nutcracker Suite, op. 71a, IIa *(Marche),* m. 1–4. (CD 5, Cut 1)

5. Moussorgsky-Ravel: Pictures at an Exhibition, Promenade II, m. 1–4. (CD 4, Cut 3)

6. Moussorgsky-Ravel: Pictures at an Exhibition, II *(Il Vecchio Castello),* m. 7–15. (CD 4, Cut 7)

7. Moussorgsky-Ravel: Pictures at an Exhibition, Promenade III, m. 1–2. (CD 4, Cut 9)

8. Tchaikovsky: Nutcracker Suite, op. 71a, IIe *(Danse Chinoise),* m. 1–4. (CD 5, Cut 5)

9. Jacob: William Byrd Suite, IV ("The Mayden's Song"), m. 1–8. (CD 3, Cut 18)

4   The Woodwinds: Intimate Colors

A.   Each of the following melodies in concert pitch have been transposed for woodwind instruments. Check the accuracy of the woodwind part and write a corrected version on the staff below of any measure with errors.

1. Holst: Second Suite in F Major, IV (Fantasia on "Dargason"), m. 1–4.

SECOND SUITE FOR BAND IN F MAJOR © Copyright 1922 by Boosey & Co., Ltd.; Copyright Renewed. Reprinted by permission of Boosey & Hawkes, Inc.

2. Mozart: Symphony in G Minor, K. 550, 1st movement, m. 56–58.

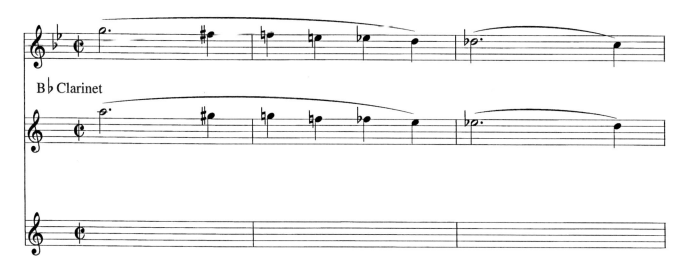

3. White: Afton Water, m. 27–30.

Neil A. Kjos Music Co., Distributor, San Diego, CA. Used by Permission, 1991.

4. Dahl: Sinfonietta for Concert Band, 1. (Introduction and Rondo), m. 6–8.

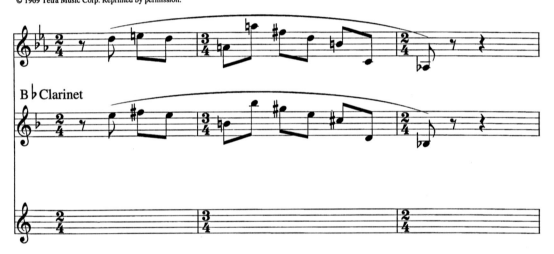

5. Dahl: Sinfonietta for Concert Band, 2. (Pastoral Nocturne), m. 35.

3. Jager: *Esprit de Corps,* m. 60–67.

Bass Clarinet

concert pitch

4. Dahl: Sinfonietta for Concert Band

B♭ Clarinet

concert pitch

5. Moussorgsky-Ravel: Pictures at an Exhibition, II *(Il Vecchio castello)*, m. 2–7.

6. White: Afton Water, m. 27–30.

7. Grainger: Lincolnshire Posy, III (Rufford Park Poachers), m. 1–6.

8. Tchaikovsky: Nutcracker Suite, op. 71a, IIc *(Danse vasse Trépak),* m. 33–40.

Bass Clarinet

concert pitch

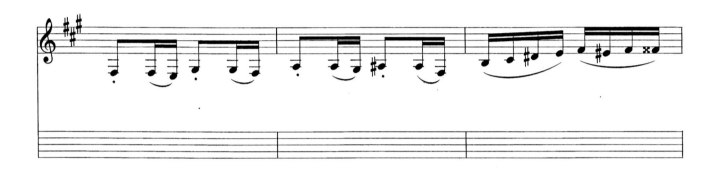

9. Mendelssohn: Calm Sea and Prosperous Voyage Overture, op. 27, m. 89–95.

Contrabassoon

concert pitch

10. Mendelssohn: Symphony no. 3 in A (Scottish), op. 56, m. 1–8.

A Clarinet

concert pitch

11. White: Afton Water, m. 98–101.

Baritone Saxophone

concert pitch

12. Jager: *Esprit de Corps,* m. 16–19.

Bassoon

concert pitch

Name_____

Date _____

2. Bartòk: Hungarian Sketches, V ("Swineherd's Dance"), m. 115–120. (CD 1, Cut 17)

3. Bizet: *Jeux d'Enfants,* op. 22, II *(Berceuse),* m. 18–30. (CD 1, Cut 19)

4. Bizet: *Jeux d'Enfants,* op. 22, III *(Impromptu),* m. 4–16. (CD 1, Cut 22)

5. Bizet: *Jeux d'Enfants,* op. 22, III *(Impromptu),* m. 67–70. (CD 1, Cut 25)

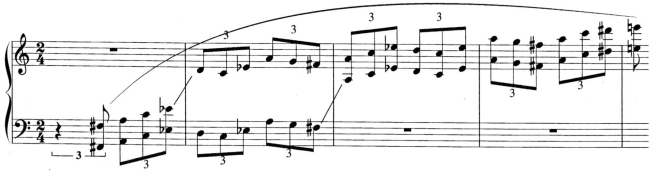

6. Bizet: *Jeux d'Enfants,* op. 22, V *(Galop),* m. 57–68. (CD 1, Cut 27)

7. Holst: First Suite in E-flat, op. 28, no. 1, I (Chaconne), m. 64–69. (CD 3, Cut 4)

FIRST SUITE IN E-FLAT FOR MILITARY BAND © Copyright 1921 by Boosey & Co., Ltd.; Copyright Renewed. Reprinted by permission of Boosey & Hawkes, Inc.

8. Mendelssohn: Fingal's Cave, op. 26, m. 70–75. (CD 3, Cut 22)

9. Mendelssohn: Fingal's Cave, op. 26, m. 263–267. (CD 3, Cut 26)

10. Moussorgsky-Ravel: Pictures at an Exhibition, Promenade II, m. 3–4. (CD 4, Cut 4)

11. Moussorgsky-Ravel: Pictures at an Exhibition, Promenade IV, m. 1-4. (CD 4, Cut 11)

F.　　　Listen again to each of the passages in section E above and identify the texture type. Remember that the condensed scores may not show all the musical materials in the passage, so you must rely on careful listening to determine the texture type. Write your answers in the blanks below:

1.　　　Bartòk: Hungarian Sketches, I ("An Evening in the Village"), m. 1–33. (CD 1, Cut 1)

2.　　　Bartòk: Hungarian Sketches, V ("Swineherd's Dance"), m. 115–120. (CD 1, Cut 17)

3.　　　Bizet: *Jeux d'Enfants,* op. 22, II (Berceuse), m. 18–30. (CD 1, Cut 19)

4.　　　Bizet: *Jeux d'Enfants,* op. 22, III (Impromptu), m. 4–16. (CD 1, Cut 22)

5.　　　Bizet: *Jeux d'Enfants*, op. 22, III (Impromptu), m. 67–70. (CD 1, Cut 25)

6.　　　Bizet: *Jeux d'Enfants,* op. 22, V (Galop), m. 60–69. (CD 1, Cut 28)

7.　　　Holst: First Suite in E-flat, op. 28, no. 1, I (Chaconne), m. 64–69. (CD 3, Cut 4)

8.　　　Mendelssohn: Fingal's Cave, op. 26, m. 70–75. (CD 3, Cut 22)

9.　　　Mendelssohn: Fingal's Cave, op. 26, m. 263–267. (CD 3, Cut 26)

10.　　Moussorgsky-Ravel: Pictures at an Exhibition, Promenade II, m. 3–4. (CD 4, Cut 3)

11.　　Moussorgsky-Ravel: Pictures at an Exhibition, Promenade IV, m. 1–4. (CD 4, Cut 11)

G.   After you have checked your answers to section E above, make a woodwind score for the following passages. Use the proper clef and transposition for each instrument. You can place two like instruments on a single staff.

1. Bartòk: Hungarian Sketches, V ("Swineherd's Dance"), m. 115–120. (CD 1, Cut 17)

2. Bizet: *Jeux d'Enfants,* op. 22, III *(Impromptu),* m. 4–16. (CD 1, Cut 22)

3. Holst: First Suite in E-flat, op. 28, no. 1, I (Chaconne), m. 64–69. (CD 3, Cut 22)

4. Moussorgksy-Ravel: Pictures at an Exhibition, Promenade II, m. 3–4. (CD 4, Cut 3)

F.   Transpose the following brass parts to concert pitch.

1. Prokofiev: Lieutenant Kijé Suite, No. V (The Burial of Kijé).

2. Jenkins: American Overture for Band

G.   Write parts for each of the following instruments so they can play the given melody in unison.

1. Tchaikovsky: Symphony No. 5 in E Minor, op. 64, II (Andante).

2. Mahler: Symphony No. 4 in G Major, I.

Name_____

Date_____

H.　　In each of the following exercises you will see a condensed score of the brass parts for a passage of orchestral or band music. Listen to the selection on the accompanying CD and identify the instrument or instruments playing each of the given lines. (In most cases there will be additional musical material played by other instruments, but concentrate your attention on the given lines, which are played by the brass.) Some lines are played by only one instrument and some by more than one. The instrumentation may change within the passage, so listen carefully for instruments entering and leaving the texture. Mark the scores to indicate the entrances and exits of each instrument as shown in chapter 4, section E on page 64.

1. Britten: The Young Person's Guide to the Orchestra, op. 34, m. 27–32. (CD 2, Cut 2)

THE YOUNG PERSON'S GUIDE TO THE ORCHESTRA © Copyright 1946 by Hawkes & Son (London) Ltd.; Copyright Renewed.
Reprinted by permission of Boosey & Hawkes, Inc.

2. Holst: First Suite in E-flat, op. 28, no. 1, I (Chaconne), m. 8–12. (CD 3, Cut 2)

FIRST SUITE IN E-FLAT FOR MILITARY BAND © Copyright 1921 by Boosey & Co., Ltd.; Copyright Renewed. Reprinted by permission of
Boosey & Hawkes, Inc.

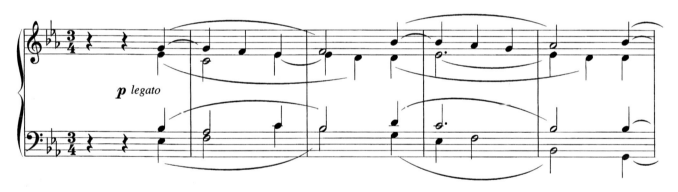

3. Holst: First Suite in E-flat, op. 28, no. 1, I (Chaconne), m. 80–92. (CD 3, Cut 5)

FIRST SUITE IN E-FLAT FOR MILITARY BAND © Copyright 1921 by Boosey & Co., Ltd.; Copyright Renewed. Reprinted by permission of
Boosey & Hawkes, Inc.

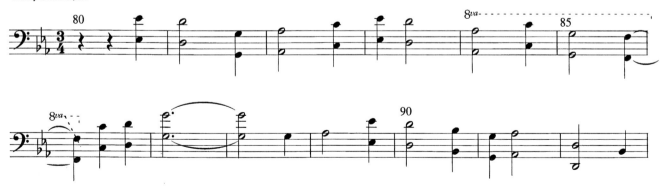

4. Holst: First Suite in E-flat, op. 28, no. 1, II (Intermezzo), m. 100–108. (CD 3, Cut 10)

5. Holst: First Suite in E-flat, op. 28, no. 1, III (March), m. 109–114. (CD 3, Cut 15)

6. Moussorgsky-Ravel: Pictures at an Exhibition, Promenade I, m. 3–4. (CD 4, Cut 2)

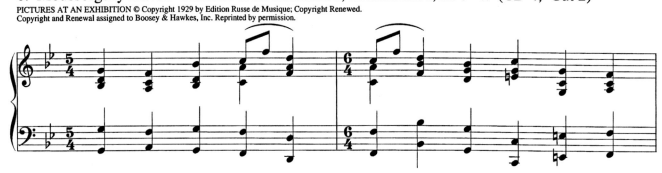

7. Tchaikovsky: Symphony No. 6 *(Pathétique),* op. 74, in B Minor, IV (Finale) m. 137–146. (CD 5, Cut 25)

I.   The following passages are similar to those in section H above, except that now the instruments may be woodwinds, brass, or a combination of the two. Listen carefully to the passages on the accompanying CD and identify the instrument or instruments playing each of the lines. Mark the scores to indicate the entrances and exits of each instrument as shown in chapter 4, section E, on page 64.

1. Holst: First Suite in E-flat, op. 28, no. 1, II (Intermezzo), m. 2–6. (CD 3, Cut 7)

FIRST SUITE IN E-FLAT FOR MILITARY BAND © Copyright 1921 by Boosey & Co., Ltd.; Copyright Renewed. Reprinted by permission of Boosey & Hawkes, Inc.

2. Mendelssohn: Overture to a Midsummer Night's Dream, op. 21, m. 222–229. (CD 3, Cut 28)

3. Mendelssohn: Fingal's Cave, op. 26, m. 185–187. (CD 3, Cut 24)

4. Tchaikovsky: Nutcracker Suite, op. 71a, IIa *(Marche),* m. 1–4. (CD 5, Cut 1)

5. Weber: Jubilee Overture, m. 9–16. (CD 5, Cut 27)

6   <u>Percussion: An Orchestra in Itself</u>

A.   The following questions pertain to the definite-pitch percussion instruments.

1.   On the staves below show the *sounding* ranges of each of the percussion instruments. (Please note that some of the percussion instruments are transposing instruments.) The resulting chart will be very helpful in gaining an understanding of the relationship among the ranges of the various definite-pitch percussion instruments.

Xylophone   Vibraphone   Orchestra bells   Chimes

Timpani   Marimba

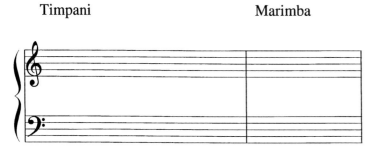

2.   Approximately how many measures rest should you allow for a timpani player to change the tuning of a single drum if the meter is $\frac{2}{4}$ and the tempo is 120 for the quarter note?

_____ to _____ measures.

3.   List the normal mallets or sticks for each of the following percussion instruments. ("Normal" in this context means the mallets or sticks the player is likely to use if no mallet preference is given in the part.)

Xylophone   _____

Marimba   _____

Timpani   _____

Chimes   _____

Orchestra bells   _____

Vibraphone   _____

4.   Which of the instruments listed in 3 above has the shortest decay time? _____

The longest? _____ Which two instruments are most nearly alike in decay time?

_____ and _____

5.   What is the purpose of the pedal mechanism on the vibraphone?

6.   What is the purpose of the fan mechanism on the vibraphone?

7.   What kind of mallets should never be used on the marimba?

B.   The following questions refer to the indefinite-pitch percussion instruments.

1.   Name the two common methods of notation for the indefinite-pitch percussion.

a.

b.

2.   What are the advantages and disadvantages of each system?

3.   Name each of the following decorations that are written for the snare drum (and sometimes other instruments as well).

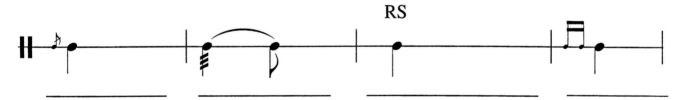

4.   Why are metal mallets never used on wooden percussion instruments?

5.   What mallets or sticks are normally used for each of the following indefinite-pitch percussion instruments? ("Normal" means the mallets or sticks the player is likely to choose when no mallet preference is indicated in the part.)

Snare drum   _____

Tambourine   _____

Woodblock   _____

Temple blocks   _____

Claves   _____

Maracas   _____

Bass drum   _____

Tom-toms   _____

Triangle   _____

Cow bells   _____

Hi-hat   _____

Crash cymbals   _____

Suspended cymbals   _____

Tamtam   _____

6.   Which indefinite-pitch percussion instrument has the shortest decay time?

7.   Which has the longest decay time?

C.   Each of the following passages is a condensed score of the percussion section for an orchestral or band composition. Listen to the passage on the accompanying CD and identify the percussion instrument (or instruments) playing each line. Mark the entrances and exits of each instrument clearly on the condensed score.

1. Hindemith: Symphony in B-flat, II *(Andantino grazioso),* m. 49–52. (CD 2, Cut 24)

2. Hindemith: Symphony in B-flat, II *(Andantino grazioso),* m. 66–71. (CD 2, Cut 25)

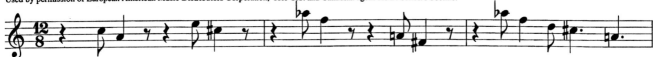

3. Britten: The Young Person's Guide to the Orchestra, op. 34, m. 375–387. (CD 2, Cut 14)

4. Jacob: William Byrd Suite, III (Jhon come kiss me now), m. 1-16. (CD 3, Cut 16)

5. Persichetti: Divertimento for Band, op. 42, VI (March), m. 1-14. (CD 4, Cut 14)

© 1951 Oliver Ditson Company. Used By Permission of The Publisher Theodore Presser Company.

6. Persichetti: Divertimento for Band, op. 42, II (Song), m. 21-31. (CD 4, Cut 13)

© 1951 Oliver Ditson Company. Used By Permission of The Publisher Theodore Presser Company.

7. Jacob: William Byrd Suite, VI (The Bells), m. 69–82. (CD 3, Cut 20)

WILLIAM BYRD SUITE. © Copyright 1924 by Boosey & Co., Copyright Renewed. Reprinted by permission of Boosey & Hawkes, Inc.

8. Hindemith-Wilson: March from Symphonic Metamorphosis, m. 1–26. (CD 2, Cut 28)

D.   Assume that you are arranging each of the following passages for band or orchestra. Create a timpani part for this arrangement, assuming the standard set of four pedal timpani. (In the Weber example, write this part on the upper of the two blank staves.) For the Weber example, listen to the passage on the accompanying CD and transcribe the timpani part on the lower of the two staves. (CD 5, cut 31) Compare the original timpani part with the part you have written. Can you account for the differences? How many timpani did Weber write for?

     1. Schubert: *Die Liebe hat gelogen,*   op. 23, no. 1, D. 751, m. 1–7.

2. Weber: Jubilee Overture, m. 356–373.

Name_____

Date _____

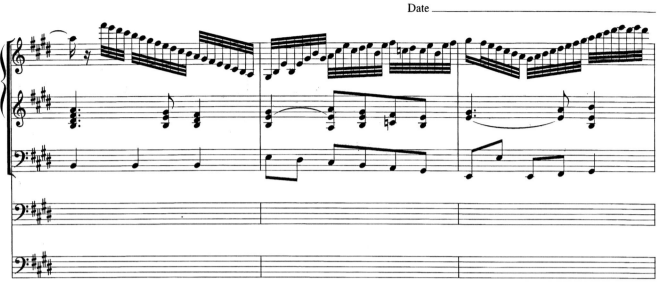

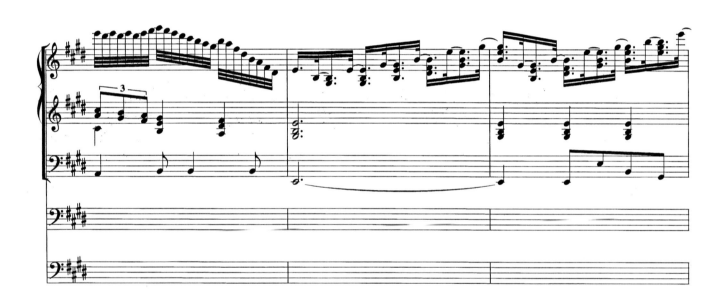

E.   Arrange the following Bach invention for an indefinite-pitch percussion duet consisting of temple blocks (percussion I) and four tom-toms (percussion II). Of course, you will not be able to express the exact pitches of the original invention, but write an arrangement that gives the listener a clear impression of the contour of the lines. Which instrument will take the upper part in the invention? Have your arrangement played by two percussionists.

Bach: Invention no. 8 in F Major, BWV 779, m. 1–15.

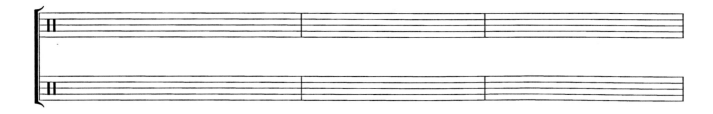

Name _____

Date _____

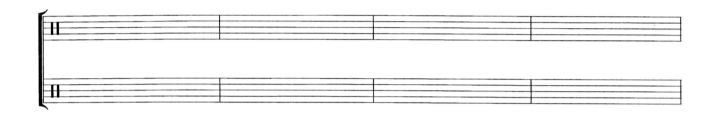

Name_____

Date_____

7   <u>Strings: Lyric Voices</u>

A.   The following exercises deal with clefs and transposition in the string family.

1.   Write parts for the viola and 'cello so they can play in unison with the violins. Use the proper clefs for each instrument.

Beethoven: Symphony No. 4 in B-flat Major, op. 60, II (Adagio), m. 2–5.

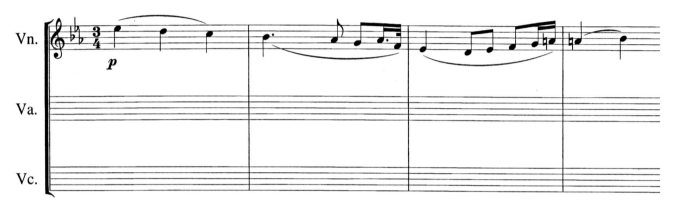

2.   Write parts for violin and 'cello so they can play in unison with the violas. Use proper clefs for each instrument.

Brahms: Academic Festival Overture, op. 80, m. 84–87.

3.   Write parts for viola and violin so they can play in unison with the 'cellos.

Ravel: Mother Goose Suite, II (Tom Thumb), m. 60–64.

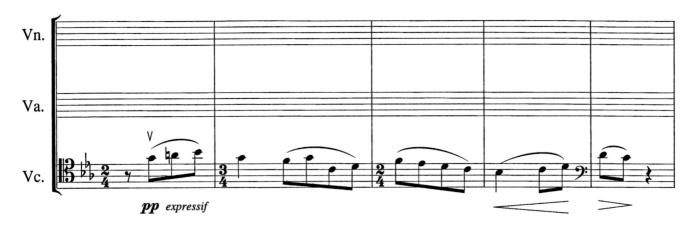

4.   Write parts for viola and double bass so they can play in unison with the 'cellos.

Mendelssohn: Overture to A Midsummer Night's Dream, op. 21, m. 146–153.

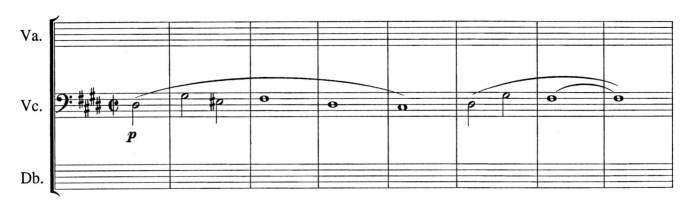

B.   Provide three different bowings for the following melodies (to be played on the violin).

Remember:

1.   The first beat of the measure is usually played with a down bow.

2.   There should be a balance between the amount of down bow and up bow.

3.   The bowing creates phrasing, and the phrasing should be logical for the melody.

4.   Slurs connect notes to be played in a single bow stroke.

1. Carissimi: *Vittoria, mio core!,* m. 26–33.

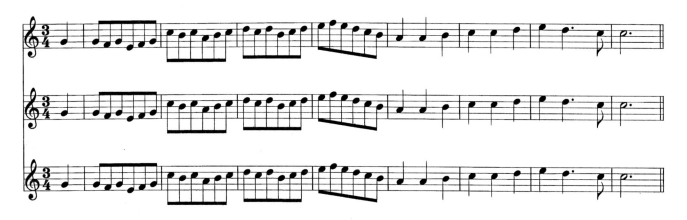

2. Grieg: Elegie, op. 47, no. 7, m. 1–8.

3. Fauré: Berceuse, op. 56, no. 1, m. 3–10.

4. Dvořák: Slavonic Dances, op. 72, no. 15, m. 13–20.

5. Beethoven: *Thema* from *Sechs Variationen* in D Major, op. 76, m. 1–8.

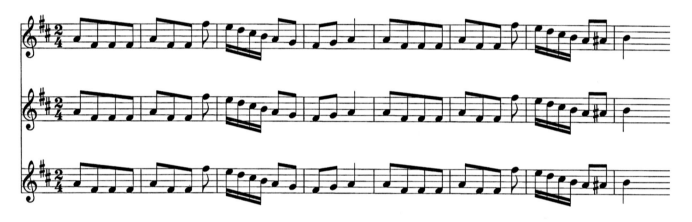

C.   Identify the string instrument playing each of the following passages:

1. Weber: Jubilee Overture, m. 91–95. (CD 5, Cut 29)

2. Bizet: *Jeux d'Enfants,* op. 22, V (Galop), m. 57–64. (CD 1, Cut 27)

3. Britten: The Young Person's Guide to the Orchestra, op. 34, m. 159–164. (CD 2, Cut 5)

4. Britten: The Young Person's Guide to the Orchestra, op. 34, m. 182–189. (CD 2, Cut 6)

THE YOUNG PERSON'S GUIDE TO THE ORCHESTRA © Copyright 1946 by Hawkes & Son (London) Ltd.; Copyright Renewed.
Reprinted by permission of Boosey & Hawkes, Inc.

5. Britten: The Young Person's Guide to the Orchestra, op. 34, m. 226–233. (CD 2, Cut 8)

THE YOUNG PERSON'S GUIDE TO THE ORCHESTRA © Copyright 1946 by Hawkes & Son (London) Ltd.; Copyright Renewed.
Reprinted by permission of Boosey & Hawkes, Inc.

D.   The following exercises contain several examples of doubling among the string instruments. Identify the instrument (or instruments) playing each of the melodies. The doubling may change, so listen carefully throughout the passage.

1. Mendelssohn: Fingal's Cave, op. 26, m. 179–182. (CD 3, Cut 23)

2. Mendelssohn: Fingal's Cave, op. 26, m. 225–228. (CD 3, Cut 25)

3. Bartók: Hungarian Sketches, III (Melody), m. 9–15. (CD 1, Cut 8)

Melody from HUNGARIAN SKETCHES © Copyright 1932 by Karl Rozsnyai and Rozsavolgyi & Co., Copyright Renewed. Copyright and Renewal
assigned to Boosey & Hawkes, Inc. Reprinted by permission.

4. Weber: Jubilee Overture, m. 50–70. (CD 5, Cut 28)

5. Tchaikovsky: *Capriccio Italien,* op. 45, m. 19–26. (CD 4, Cut 23)

6. Tchaikovsky: *Capriccio Italien,* op. 45, m. 229–232. (CD 4, Cut 25)

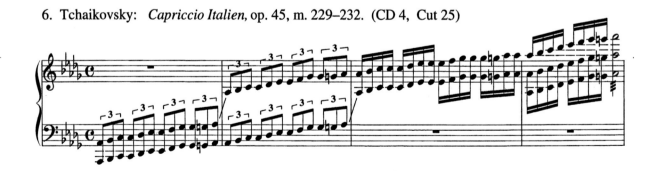

7. Tchaikovsky: *Capriccio Italien,* op. 45, m. 281–288. (CD 4, Cut 27)

E.   The following are examples of various special effects on the strings. Identify the special effect and rewrite the line on the staff below to show the proper notation for the special effect. (Note that only the pitches and rhythms are given in these examples, not the correct notation for the special effect.)

1. Bartók: Hungarian Sketches, I ("An Evening in the Village"), m. 10–13. (CD 1, Cut 2)

An Evening in the Village from HUNGARIAN SKETCHES © Copyright 1932 by Karl Rozsnyai and Rozsavolgyi & Co., Copyright Renewed. Copyright and Renewal assigned to Boosey & Hawkes, Inc. Reprinted by permission.

2. Bartók: Hungarian Sketches, V ("Swineherd's Dance"), m. 96–111. (CD 1, Cut 16)

Swineherd's Dance from HUNGARIAN SKETCHES © Copyright 1932 by Karl Rozsnyai and Rozsavolgyi & Co., Copyright Renewed. Copyright and Renewal assigned to Boosey & Hawkes, Inc. Reprinted by permission.

3. Bizet: *Jeux d'Enfants,* op. 22, II *(Berceuse),* m. 1–5. (CD 1, Cut 18)

4. Britten: The Young Person's Guide to the Orchestra, op. 34, m. 70–77. (CD 2, Cut 3)

THE YOUNG PERSON'S GUIDE TO THE ORCHESTRA © Copyright 1946 by Hawkes & Son (London) Ltd.; Copyright Renewed.
Reprinted by permission of Boosey & Hawkes, Inc.

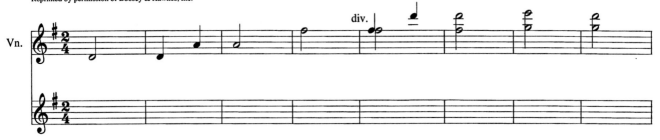

5. Ravel: Pavane for a Dead Princess, m. 1–7. (CD 4, Cut 6)

6. Tchaikovsky: Romeo and Juliet Overture, m. 86–90. (CD 5, Cut 13)

7. Tchaikovsky: Romeo and Juliet Overture, m. 192–196. (CD 5, Cut 16)

8   Keyboard Instruments, Harp, and Guitars

A.   Add accidentals to the given scale to show the tuning indicated by each of the following harp pedal settings. Review the order of the pedals and the three pedal positions as needed to complete this problem.

1.

2.

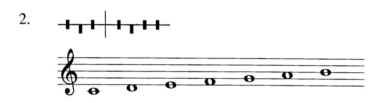

3.

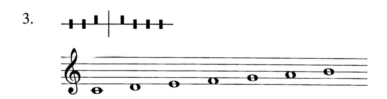

4.

5.

B.   The following three passages from the literature have no pedal indications. A change in the pedals is needed each time the pedal chart appears above the score. Indicate the correct pedal positions throughout each passage, including the initial setting. Review the order of the pedals and the three pedal positions as needed to complete this problem.

1. Ravel: *Pavane pour une infante défunte,* m. 50–55. (CD 4, Cut 18)

2. Tchaikovsky: *Capriccio Italien,* op. 45, m. 226–229. (CD 4, Cut 24)

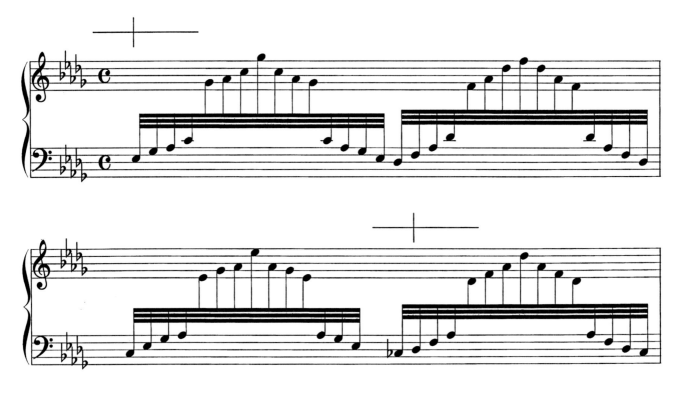

3. Ravel: *Pavane pour une infante défunte,* m. 60–72. (CD 4, Cut 19)

C.   Complete the pedal charts below so that the harp will produce the indicated chord as a glissando. Remember that each of the strings must be tuned to a chord tone (or its enharmonic equivalent) to produce the given chord as a glissando. You may use the staff below to work out the proper tuning for each of the seven strings that the harp has in each octave.

D.   Write a piano part for the opening section the allegro of Haydn's London Symphony, shown below in condensed score. The piano part should have the important elements of the texture (PM, SM, HRS, etc.) and provide support that would allow the work to be played by a young orchestra with incomplete instrumentation. The part should be playable by a pianist of moderate ability. Write your piano part on the blank staves on the following page.

Hadyn: Symphony no. 104 in D Major (London), I (Adagio-Allegro)

Haydn: Symphony no. 104 in D Major (London), I (Adagio-Allegro)

Allegro

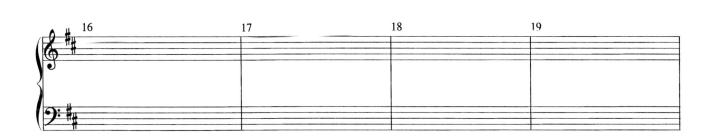

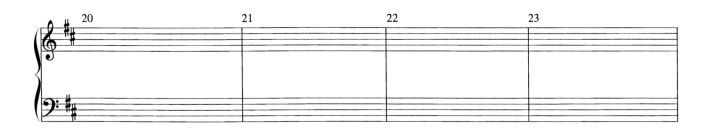

9   <u>Writing for Younger Musicians</u>

A.   Rewrite each of the following passages for the instrumentalists indicated on the staves below. Consider the key, meter, range, and difficulty of rhythmic patterns and alter as needed to bring the passage within the playing ability of the young musician, while maintaining as much of the character of the original material as possible.

1. Beethoven: Symphony no. 2 in D Major, op. 36, II (Larghetto), m. 1–8.

2. Haydn: Symphony no. 92 in G Major (Oxford), II (Adagio), m. 1–4.

3. Brahms: Variations on a Theme by Joseph Haydn, op. 56a, VII (Grazioso), m. 1–6.

4. Schubert: Symphony in C Major, op. posth., II (Andante con moto), m. 8–16.

high school B♭ Trumpet

elementary B♭ Clarinet

(Tpt.)

(Cl.)

5. Haydn: Symphony no. 100 in G Major, II (Allegretto), m. 1–8

elementary Flute

elementary 'Cello

(Fl.)

(Vc.)

6. Weber: Overture to *Preciosa,* m. 1–8.

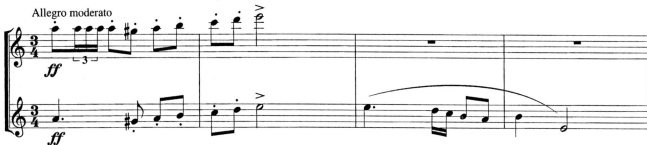

junior high Flute and B♭ Clarinet

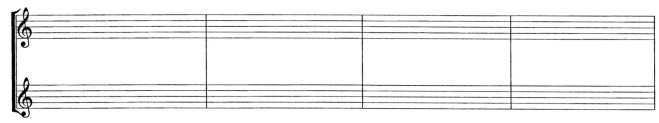

high school B♭ Trumpet and Horn

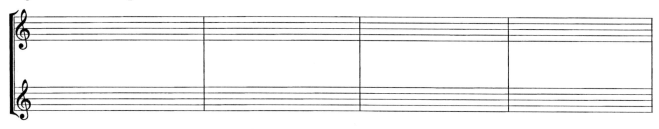

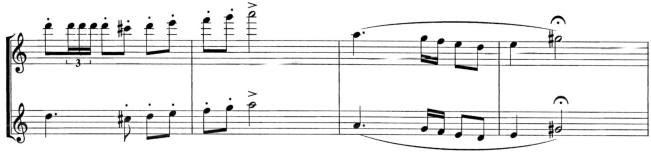

(Fl., Cl.)

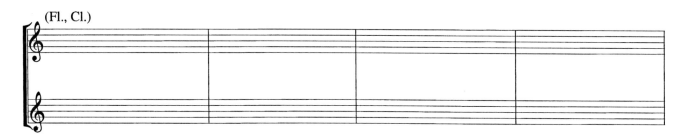

(Tpt., Hn.)

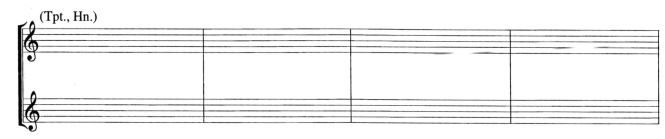

7. Beethoven: Symphony no. 1 in C Major, op. 21, II (Andante), m. 1–7

elementary Violin

elementary B♭ Trumpet

elementary Flute

elementary Horn

B.   Examine each of the following melodies and indicate in the boxes below which players could easily play the passage. If younger musicians could not be expected to play the passage, describe the difficulties in the space below the boxes. Compare your answers with those of your classmates and discuss the potential difficulties in class.

1. German folk song—B♭ Trumpet

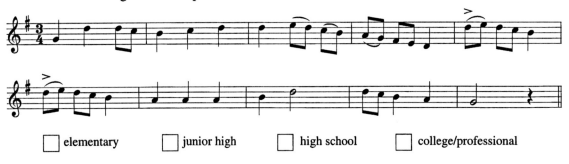

☐ elementary   ☐ junior high   ☐ high school   ☐ college/professional

Difficulties:

2. British folk song—Oboe

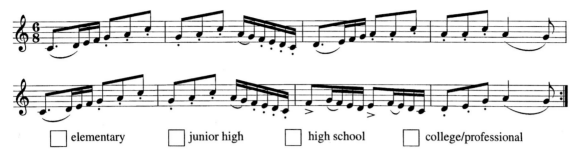

☐ elementary   ☐ junior high   ☐ high school   ☐ college/professional

Difficulties:

3. Croatian folk song—Violin

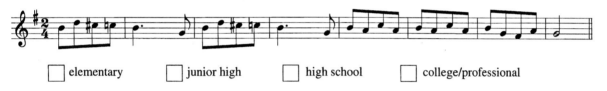

☐ elementary   ☐ junior high   ☐ high school   ☐ college/professional

Difficulties:

4. German folk song—B♭ Clarinet

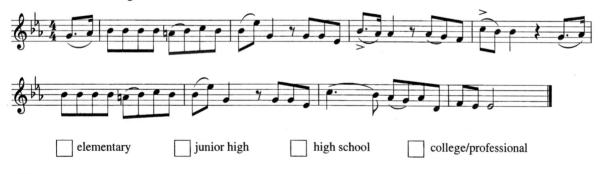

☐ elementary   ☐ junior high   ☐ high school   ☐ college/professional

Difficulties:

5. Swedish folk song—Violin

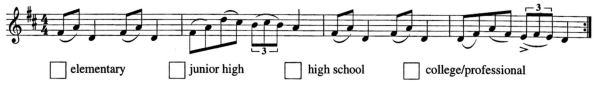

☐ elementary ☐ junior high ☐ high school ☐ college/professional

Difficulties:

6. Bohemian folk song—Horn

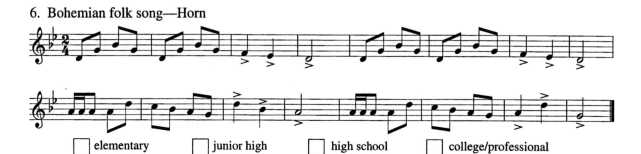

☐ elementary ☐ junior high ☐ high school ☐ college/professional

Difficulties:

7. Hungarian folk song—Trombone

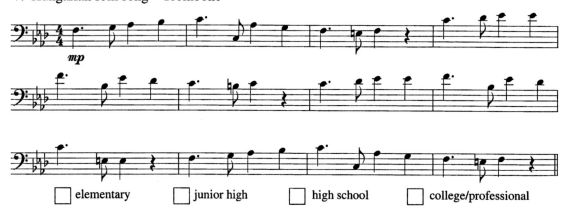

☐ elementary ☐ junior high ☐ high school ☐ college/professional

Difficulties:

Name________________________

Date ________________________

8. German folk song—Tuba

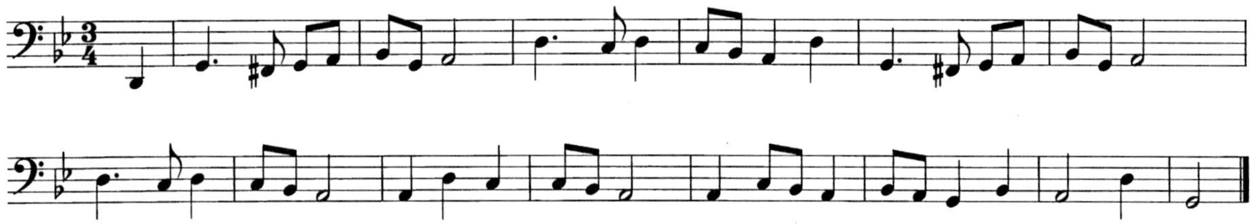

☐ elementary ☐ junior high ☐ high school ☐ college/professional

Difficulties:

9. French folk song—Flute

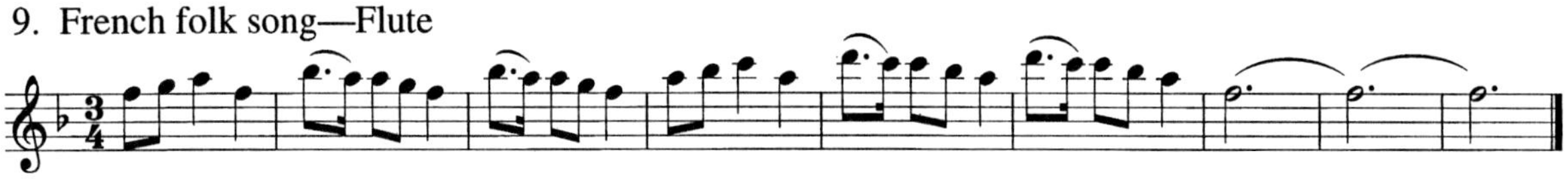

☐ elementary ☐ junior high ☐ high school ☐ college/professional

Difficulties:

10. British folk song—'Cello

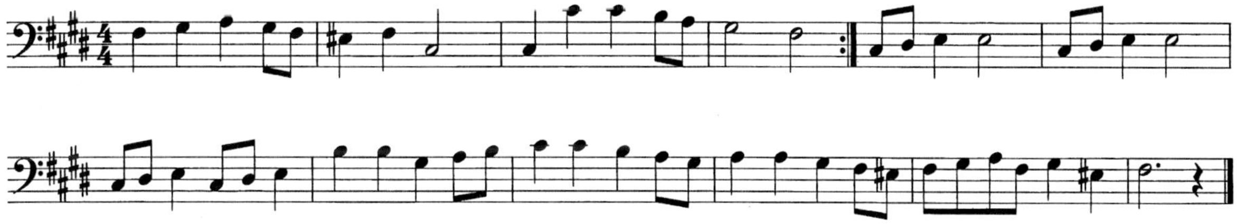

☐ elementary ☐ junior high ☐ high school ☐ college/professional

Difficulties:

11. French folk song—Double Bass

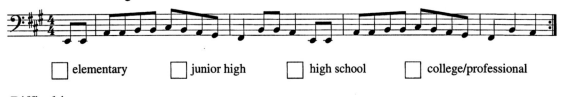

☐ elementary   ☐ junior high   ☐ high school   ☐ college/professional

Difficulties:

12. French folk song—Alto Saxophone

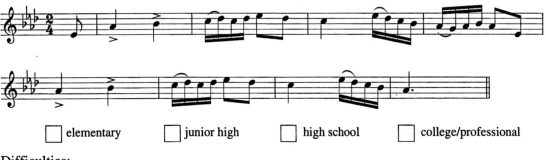

☐ elementary   ☐ junior high   ☐ high school   ☐ college/professional

Difficulties:

13. Polish folk song—Bassoon

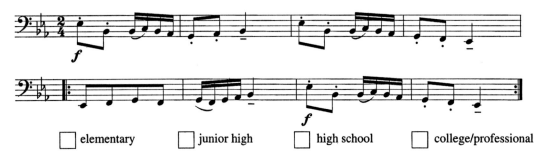

☐ elementary   ☐ junior high   ☐ high school   ☐ college/professional

Difficulties:

10   Balance, Blend, Masking, and Voice Crossing

A.   Consider each of the following scale passages that have been scored for two instruments (one player on each part) and make an estimate of any balance or blend problems that might occur anywhere in the passage. You should not assume that every example has balance or blend problems. Play the examples in class, if the instruments are available, and determine if your estimates were accurate.

1.

Balance problems:

Blend problems:

2.

Balance problems:

Blend problems:

3.

Balance problems:

Blend problems:

4.

E♭ Alto Sax.

Bari. Sax.

Balance problems:

Blend problems:

5.

B♭ Tpt.

Tbn.

Balance problems:

Blend problems:

6.

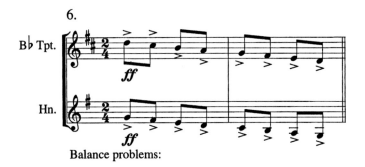

B♭ Tpt.

Hn.

Balance problems:

Blend problems:

7.

Hn.

Bsn.

Balance problems:

Blend problems:

8.

Balance problems:

Blend problems:

9.

Balance problems:

Blend problems:

10.

Balance problems:

Blend problems:

11.

Balance problems:

Blend problems:

12.

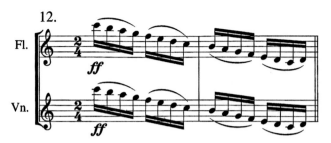

Balance problems:

Blend problems:

13.

Balance problems:

Blend problems:

14.

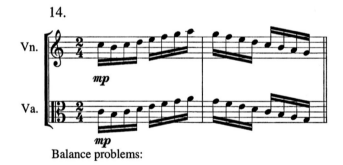

Balance problems:

Blend problems:

15.

Balance problems:

Blend problems:

B.   Examine each of the following chords and note potential problems of blend or balance that may occur, assuming that the chords should blend and balance perfectly. Some chords may have no problems in blend or balance. Play the examples in class, if the instruments are available, and determine if your estimates were accurate.

1.

Balance problems:

Blend problems:

2.

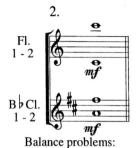

Balance problems:

Blend problems:

3.

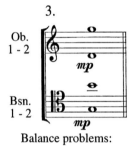

Balance problems:

Blend problems:

4.

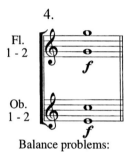

Balance problems:

Blend problems:

5.

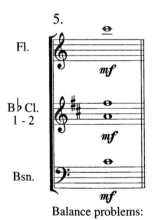

Balance problems:

Blend problems:

6.

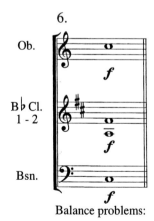

Balance problems:

Blend problems:

7.

Fl.

Ob.
1 - 2

Cl.

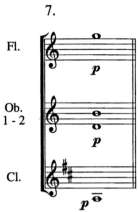

Balance problems:

Blend problems:

8.

B♭ Tpt.
1 - 2

Hns.
1 - 2

Tbns.
1 - 2 - 3

Balance problems:

Blend problems:

9.

Flutes
1 - 2 - 3

Balance problems:

Blend problems:

10.

Cl.
1 - 2 - 3

Balance problems:

Blend problems:

11.

Hns.
1-2-3-4

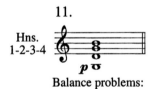

Balance problems:

Blend problems:

12.

B♭
Tpts.
1 - 2 - 3

Balance problems:

Blend problems:

13.

Bb
Tpts.
1 - 2 - 3

Balance problems:

Blend problems:

14.

Bb Cl.
1 - 2 - 3

Balance problems:

Blend problems:

15.

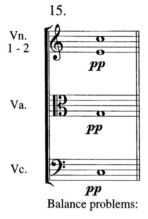

Vn.
1 - 2

Va.

Vc.

Balance problems:

Blend problems:

16.

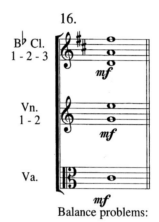

Bb Cl.
1 - 2 - 3

Vn.
1 - 2

Va.

Balance problems:

Blend problems:

11   Scoring Monophonic Textures and Melodic Lines

A.   Transcribe the given folk songs for three to five instruments as assigned by your instructor. The transcription must maintain the monophonic texture of the original, but various octave and unison doublings are allowed and encouraged. The melodies may be transposed as needed for the instruments. Note that there are no tempos, dynamics, or articulations in the original melodies. The editing must be created as a part of the transcription process. The orchestration should be varied from phrase to phrase to provide contrast in color. Use the scoring of "Greensleeves" in the chapter as a model for your transcriptions.

1. Irish folk song

2. British folk song

3. Hungarian folk song

4. Polish folk song

B.   Listen to the following brief monophonic passages and identify the instruments used. The instrumentation may change within the passage so listen carefully.

1. Bartók: Hungarian Sketches I ("An Evening in the Village"), m. 42–44. (CD 1, Cut 4)
An Evening in the Village from HUNGARIAN SKETCHES © Copyright 1932 by Karl Rozsnyai and Rozsavolgyi & Co., Copyright Renewed. Copyright and Renewal assigned to Boosey & Hawkes, Inc. Reprinted by permission.

2. Bizet: *Jeux d'Enfants,* op. 22, V (Galop), m. 121–124. (CD 1, Cut 31)

3. Holst: First Suite in E-flat for Military Band, op. 28, no. 1, I (Chaconne), m. 1–8. (CD 3, Cut 1)
FIRST SUITE IN E-FLAT FOR MILITARY BAND © Copyright 1921 by Boosey & Co., Ltd.; Copyright Renewed. Reprinted by permission of Boosey & Hawkes, Inc.

4. Tchaikovsky: *Capriccio Italien,* op. 45, m. 1–7. (CD 4, Cut 21)

5. Tchaikovsky: *Capriccio Italien,* op. 45, m. 445–454. (CD 4, Cut 28)

6. Jacob: William Byrd Suite, IV (The Mayden's Song), m. 1–4. (CD 3, Cut 18)
WILLIAM BYRD SUITE. © Copyright 1924 by Boosey & Co., Copyright Renewed. Reprinted by permission of Boosey & Hawkes, Inc.

Name_____

Date_____

7. Tchaikovsky: Romeo and Juliet Overture, m. 365–367. (CD 5, Cut 17)

8. Tchaikovsky: Romeo and Juliet Overture, m. 479–484. (CD 5, Cut 18)

C.   The following melodic lines are the PMs in passages in a variety of texture types. Identify the instrument or instruments assigned to these lines, ignoring the surrounding textural elements. The instrumentation may change within the passage so listen carefully.

1. Weber: Jubilee Overture, m. 104–111. (CD 5, Cut 30)

2. Tchaikovsky: Nutcracker Suite, op. 71a, III ("Waltz of the Flowers"), m. 142–148. (CD 5, Cut 10)

3. Ravel: *Pavane pour une Infante Défunte,* m. 28–39. (CD 4, Cut 17)

4. Holst: First Suite in E-flat for Military Band, op. 28, no. 1, I (Chaconne), m. 64–100.
(CD 3, Cut 4)

FIRST SUITE IN E-FLAT FOR MILITARY BAND © Copyright 1921 by Boosey & Co., Ltd.; Copyright Renewed. Reprinted by permission of
Boosey & Hawkes, Inc.

5. Holst: First Suite in E-flat for Military Band, op. 28, no. 1, II (Intermezzo), m. 84–91.
(CD 3, Cut 9)
FIRST SUITE IN E-FLAT FOR MILITARY BAND © Copyright 1921 by Boosey & Co., Ltd.; Copyright Renewed. Reprinted by permission of
Boosey & Hawkes, Inc.

6. Holst: First Suite in E-flat for Military Band, op. 28, no. 1, II (Intermezzo), m. 100–127.
(CD 3, Cut 10)
FIRST SUITE IN E-FLAT FOR MILITARY BAND © Copyright 1921 by Boosey & Co., Ltd.; Copyright Renewed. Reprinted by permission of
Boosey & Hawkes, Inc.

7. Mendelssohn: Incidental Music to "A Midsummer Night's Dream", op. 61, V (Intermezzo), m. 1–10. (CD 3, Cut 29)

8. Bizet: *Jeux d'Enfants,* op. 22, II (Berceuse), m. 18–26. (CD 1, Cut 20)

12   Scoring Homorhythmic Textures and Harmony

A.   Score the following example of homorhythmic texture for ensembles assigned by your instructor. Transpose these excerpts as needed to accommodate the ranges and favorite keys of the instruments. These passages may be scored as they appear or be expanded through octave doubling. Use the various scorings of "America" in the book as a guide. Notice that tempos, dynamics, and articulations are missing from these passages and must be supplied by you. Play your transcriptions in class and compare various settings in terms of musical effectiveness.

1. Schumann: *Freudich sehr, o meine Seele* (Rejoice, O My Soul), m. 1–8.

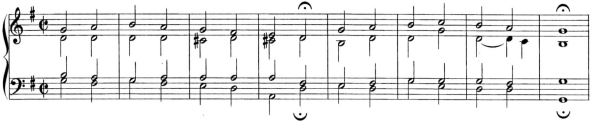

2. Mason: "Joy to the World!", m. 1–7.

3. Bach: *Jesu, du mein liebstes Leben* (Jesus, Thou My Dearest Life), m. 1–8.

4. Grieg: *Matrosenlied,* op. 68, no. 1, m. 1–8.

B.   Listen to the following homorhythmic passages and identify the instruments assigned to each part. In heavier textures, with extensive doubling, you may not be able to identify all the instruments or decide which part they are playing, but do your best with each passage. The instrumentation may change within the passage.

1. Tchaikovsky: Romeo and Juliet Overture, m. 1–10. (CD 5, Cut 12)

2. Tchaikovsky: Romeo and Juliet Overture, m. 112–115. (CD 5, Cut 14)

3. Tchaikovsky: *Capriccio Italien,* op. 45, m. 8–15. (CD 4, Cut 22)

4. Persichetti: Divertimento for Band, op. 42, VI (March), m. 9–12. (CD 4, Cut 15)

© 1951 Oliver Ditson Company. Used By Permission of The Publisher Theodore Presser Company.

5. Tchaikovsky: Nutcracker Suite, op. 71a, IIa *(Marche),* m. 1–4. (CD 5, Cut 1)

6. Tchaikovsky: Nutcracker Suite, op. 71a, III *(Valse des Fleurs),* m. 1–4. (CD 5, Cut 6)

7. Holst: First Suite in E-flat for Military Band, op. 28, no. 1, III (March), m. 12–16. (CD 3, Cut 14)

FIRST SUITE IN E-FLAT FOR MILITARY BAND © Copyright 1921 by Boosey & Co., Ltd.; Copyright Renewed. Reprinted by permission of Boosey & Hawkes, Inc.

13   **Scoring Polyphonic Textures**

A.   Score each of the following excerpts for instruments assigned by your instructor. Follow the process outlined in chapter 13 and summarized on page 237. You can do your analysis and plan the transcription in this book, but you will need to produce the score and parts on your own paper or with a computer.

1. Haydn: String Quartet, op. 76, no. 6, mvt. 1.

2. Bach: Invention no. 11 from 15 Two-Part Inventions, BWV 782, m. 1–6.

3. Bach: Fugue VII from the Art of the Fugue, BWV 1080, m. 1–5.

4. Palestrina: *In Festo Transfigurationis Domini,* m. 1–10.

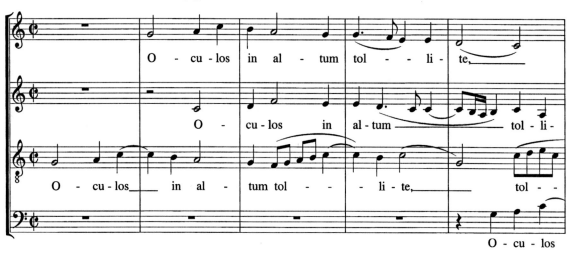

B.   Listen carefully to each of the following excerpts and name the instrument or instruments playing each line. The instrumentation may change within the excerpt, so listen carefully. Which lines are PMs and which are SMs? How does the composer make this clear in the orchestration? Do the instruments balance? Do they blend?

1. Britten: The Young Person's Guide to the Orchestra, op. 34, m. 444–477. (CD 2, Cut 18)

2. Jacob: William Byrd Suite, III ("Jhon come kiss me now"), m. 41–44. (CD 3, Cut 17)

3. Jacob: William Byrd Suite, VI ("The Bells"), m. 1–11. (CD 3, Cut 19)

4. Holst: First Suite in E-flat for Military Band, op. 28, no. 1, I (Chaconne), m. 23–31. (CD 3, Cut 3)

5. Holst: First Suite in E-flat for Military Band, op. 28, no. 1, I (Chaconne), m. 64–72.
(CD 3, Cut 4)

FIRST SUITE IN E-FLAT FOR MILITARY BAND © Copyright 1921 by Boosey & Co., Ltd.; Copyright Renewed. Reprinted by permission of
Boosey & Hawkes, Inc.

6. Mendelssohn: Symphony no. 4 in A Major (Italian), op. 90, II (Andante con moto),
m. 1–7. (CD 3, Cut 31)

A.   Separate the textural elements in each of the following examples of homophonic texture using the methods suggested in chapter 14 and summarized on page 256 of the text. Pay particular attention to possible SM elements that may only be implied in the original texture. Sketch out a possible accompaniment texture that will resemble the original but be idiomatic for an orchestra or band. You may choose the medium in each case but be sure that you do some examples for each medium. Show your solutions in class and discuss the relative merits of various approaches to the accompaniment textures.

Select one or more of the excerpts and write a complete transcription for an ensemble assigned by your instructor. Produce a finished score and parts and play the transcription(s) in class.

1. Chopin: Nocturne, op. 48, no. 1, m. 1–8.

2. Kabalevsky: Toccatina, op. 27, m. 1-13.

From MUSIC FOR ANALYSIS, Second Edition, by Thomas Benjamin, Michael Horvit, and Robert Nelson © 1984 by Houghton Mifflin Company. Reprinted by permission of Wadsworth, Inc.

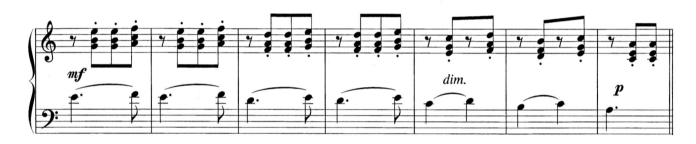

3. Mozart: Piano Sonata, K. 283 (first movement), m. 1–10.

4. Schubert: Waltz.

5. Beethoven: Piano Sonata in C Minor *(Pathétique),* op. 13 (second movement), m. 1–8.

Name_____

Date_____

6. Haydn: Piano Sonata in D Major, Hob. XVI:19, (3rd movement), m. 61–67.

7. Beethoven: Piano Sonata in G Major, op. 49, no. 2 (2nd movement), m. 1–8.

Tempo di Menuetto (♩ = 112)

Scoring Homophonic Textures: Melody and Accompaniment   145

8. Haydn: Piano Sonata no. 25 (1st movement), m. 25–36.

9. Chopin: Nocturne, op. 9, no. 1.

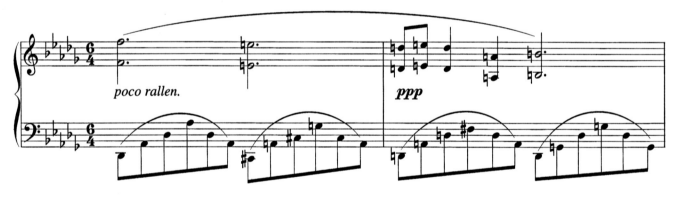

B.   Listen carefully to each of the following excerpts and name the instrument or instruments playing each part. The instrumentation may change within the excerpt, so listen carefully. Do a textural analysis of the excerpt. How does the composer keep the melodic lines and accompaniment figures clear and distinct in the orchestration? Consider factors of balance and blend in answering this question.

1. Tchaikovsky: Romeo and Juliet Overture, m. 184–192. (CD 5, cut 15)

2. Tchaikovsky: *Capriccio Italien,* op. 45, m. 233–237. (CD 4, cut 26)

3. White: Afton Water, m. 18–21. (CD 5, Cut 35)

4. White: Afton Water, m. 56–59. (CD 5, Cut 36)

5. Mendelssohn: Fingal's Cave, op. 26, m. 179–182. (CD 3, Cut 23)

6. Bartók: Hungarian Sketches, I ("An Evening in the Village"), m. 10–13. (CD 1, Cut 2)

7. Bartók: Hungarian Sketches, III (Melody), m. 32–35. (CD 1, Cut 9)

8. **Moussorgsky-Ravel:** Pictures at an Exhibition, II *(Il Vecchio Castello),* m. 7–12. (CD 4, Cut 5)

9. **Haydn:** Symphony no. 104 in D Major, Hob. 1/104 (London), I (Allegro), m. 130–137. (CD 2, Cut 21)

10. **Weber:** Jubilee Overture, m. 104–110. (CD 5, Cut 30)

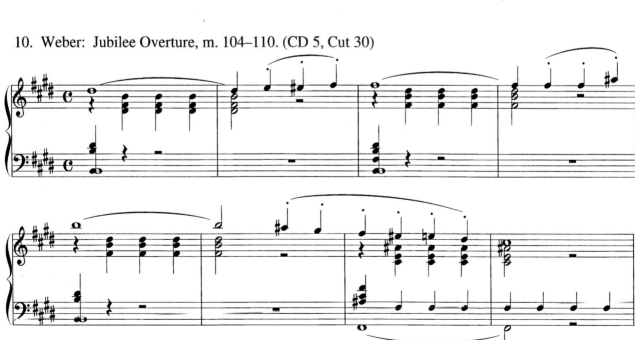

11. Tchaikovsky: Nutcracker Suite, op. 71a, III *(Valse des Fleurs),* m. 204–210. (CD 5, Cut 11)

15   Creating Accompaniment Textures

A.   Create accompaniments for the following short excerpts from Brahms songs, using the given harmonizations (taken from the original songs). Establish a rhythmic motive, sketch in an accompaniment, consider secondary melodies, and write a finished accompaniment. Then check your accompaniment with the texture Brahms provided. How do your accompaniments resemble Brahms's textures, and how are they different? (Notice Brahms's predilection for low, dark sonorities.) Study Brahms's accompaniments to see how they could have been created using the techniques outlined in the chapter.

1. Brahms: *Alte Liebe,* op. 72, no. 1, m. 2-5.

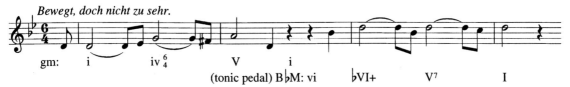

2. Brahms: *Erinnerung,* op. 63, no. 2, m. 1-8.

3. Brahms: *O liebliche Wangen,* op. 47, no. 4, m. 1-4.

4. Brahms: *Wie Melodien zieht es mir,* op. 105, no. 1, m. 1-5.

B.   Provide a harmonization for the folk songs below. Create accompaniment textures for each using the technique described in chapter 15 of the text and summarized on p. 269. Play the finished products in class and compare your harmonization and accompaniment textures with those of the other students.

1. German folk song

2. Swedish folk song

3. German folk song

4. French folk song

5. German folk song

6. Polish folk song

7. German folk song

16   <u>Writing Introductions, Transitions, and Codas</u>

A.   Identify at least ten melodic motives in the following melody. Mark the motives with brackets and label with letters as shown in figure 16.12 (p. 285) in the book.

Russian folk song

B.   Choose eight of your melodic motives and develop sequences from them. For examples, see figure 16.13 (p. 286) in the book. Label each of your sequences to show the motive from which it is derived.

1. motive _____

2. motive _____

3. motive _____

4. motive _____

5. motive _____

6. motive _____

7. motive _____

8. motive _____

C.   Choose one of the folk song settings you completed in section B in this workbook (p. 151). Develop an introduction at least four measures in length for this melody, using the accompaniment texture as a basis. Follow the step-by-step approach described in the summary on p. 287 of the book at the beginning, but bear in mind that you may find some variation in the outline works best for you. The end result is more important than your process of arriving at it. You will need your own music paper to complete this project.

D.   Choose a second folk song setting from section B and write a transition between the folk song you were working with in section C above and this song. Transpose this setting if necessary. Make your transition at least four measures in length. Follow the step-by-step approach, or a variation that you find more convenient for you. You might experiment with a different approach to this problem than you used for the introduction above. Again, the end result is more important than the process.

E.   Write a coda to follow the second folk song in section D above, using similar techniques and experimenting with variations to your approach.

F.   A short arrangement can be assembled from your settings and the introduction, transition, and coda you wrote in sections C, D, and E. Complete this brief arrangement and score it for an ensemble that is available to you.

Name_____

Date_____

17   Planning the Form: Tonal Plan of an Arrangement

In this chapter we will plan the form of an arrangement that will be completed in chapter 18. The process is described in detail in the summary on p. 295 of the book. Decide before you begin about the medium and age level for which you will be writing. It is important that you choose, if possible, a medium that you will have available for a reading of the completed work.

1.   Select two or three themes that you will use. You may use melodies from this workbook or select your own. See "An Example of Formal Planning" on p. 290 of the book for a discussion of important factors in choosing a theme. Also consult items (1) and (2) in the summary on p. 295–96. Submit your themes to your instructor for discussion and approval before continuing with this exercise.

2.   Choose the order of the themes and select the keys, referring to "The Order of the Themes" on p. 292 and "Key Relationships Between Themes" on p. 297. Also consider items (3), (4), and (5) from the summary on p. 295 in completing this step.

3.   Determine the need for introduction, transitions, and coda, referring to "Introduction, Transitions, and Coda" on p. 293. Also consider items (6), (7), (8), and (9) from the summary on p. 297. Your plan must include a coda and at least two other sections (introduction and transitions).

4.   Plan the tension curve for the arrangement, referring to "Planning for the Climax" and "Planning the Tension Curve of the Arrangement," on p. 294. Also consider items (10), (11), and (12) from the summary on p. 295.

5.   Draw a chart of your arrangement similar to figure 17.6 and add the keys of all sections to the chart. Submit this chart along with your themes to your instructor for approval. Be careful to label your themes to match the labels on the chart.

In this chapter you will complete the arrangement you planned in chapter 17. You will use all the skills you have developed in this course and see the results of your work in a completed arrangement. It is important that you have an opportunity to hear a reading of your arrangement, since a performance is the best means of testing the effectiveness of any arrangement. Bear in mind that an ensemble's first attempt at a performance is not in any way representative of the way a well-rehearsed performance will sound, but much can be gained nevertheless.

1.   First concentrate your attention on the themes and produce a good accompaniment for each, or rework the given accompaniment if the theme already has an accompaniment. Consider the level of performer in writing the accompaniment and use the methods developed in chapter 15 in writing the accompaniment.

2.   Next write the connecting sections (introduction, transitions, and coda) using the methods developed in chapter 16. Consider the tension curve you developed in your plan when writing these sections, but bear in mind that this plan is not "carved in stone" and may change as the arrangement develops.

3.   Now you are ready to put your arrangement together. It is best to write a condensed score in concert pitch at first. When you have much more experience, you may be able to skip this step, but don't be tempted to do so this first time, even if the amount of writing seems overwhelming. Plan times to work on the condensed score over several days and you will find that with regular, methodical work the score pages pile up!

4.   Finally, produce the full score and parts and get a reading. This step will use all your accumulated skills. The end result is a piece of music that you can be proud to claim as your own. I hope this piece is the first of many that you will create as an arranger. If you look around, you will find many opportunities to use your skills and develop your technique.

19   Special Considerations for Jazz Ensemble

A.   The following portion of a lead sheet has been transposed for several wind instruments.

     Check the accuracy of the wind instrument parts and write corrected versions of any measures with error on the staves below.

concert pitch

Examine the instrumental parts (as you corrected them above) and describe any performance difficulties you detect.

Trumpet:

Trombone:

Alto Saxophone:

B.   Write the following chord progression in the key of G major as a chord chart in $\frac{4}{4}$ meter for (1) piano and for (2) alto saxophone, using standard jazz notation (virgules and chord symbols):

G major 7 (4 beats)

F-sharp minor 7; flatted 5th (2 beats)

B 7, flatted ninth (2 beats)

E minor 7 (2 beats)

E-flat diminished 7 (2 beats)

D minor 7 (2 beats)

G 9, augmented 5th (2 beats)

C major 7 (4 beats)

C-sharp minor 7, flatted 5th (2 beats)

F-sharp 7, flatted ninth (2 beats)

B major 7 (2 beats)

G-sharp minor 7 (2 beats)

A minor 7 (2 beats)

D 7 added 6th, flatted 9th (2 beats)

G major 7 (4 beats)

Name_____

Date _____

1. Piano

2. Alto Saxophone

Transpose the chord progression above to the key of B-flat major and write chord charts for (3) flute and (4) trumpet on the staves below.

3. Flute

4. Trumpet

Transpose the chord progression on the previous page to the key of C major and write chord charts for (5) trombone and (6) baritone saxophone on the staves below.

5. Trombone

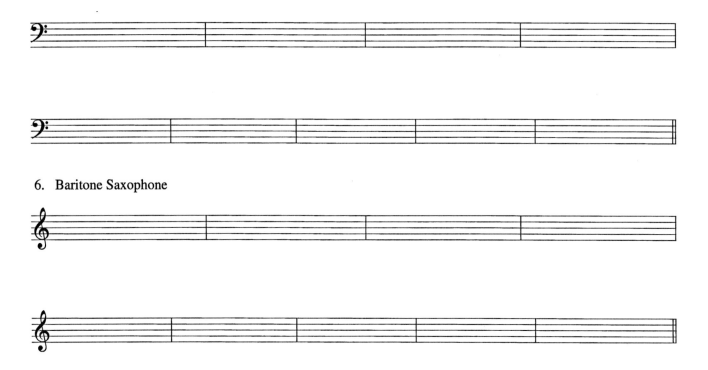

6. Baritone Saxophone

C.   Rewrite the following four-bar rock-style passage in C major as eight measures of $\frac{2}{2}$ meter swing in D-flat major (hint: double all note and rest values).

Write parts for (1) trombone and (2) tenor saxophone for the swing passage you wrote in above. Use the middle register of each instrument.

1. Trombone

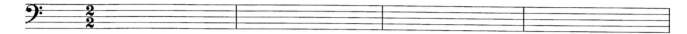

2. Tenor Saxophone

D.   Rewrite the following eight-measure, $\frac{2}{2}$ rock-style passage in the key of F major as four measures of half-time, $\frac{4}{4}$ meter rock in the key of B-flat major (hint: halve all the note and rest values; two measures reduce to one).

Write parts for (1) baritone saxophone and (2) trumpet for the half-time passage you wrote above. Use the middle register of baritone saxophone and the upper register of the trumpet.

1. Baritone Saxophone

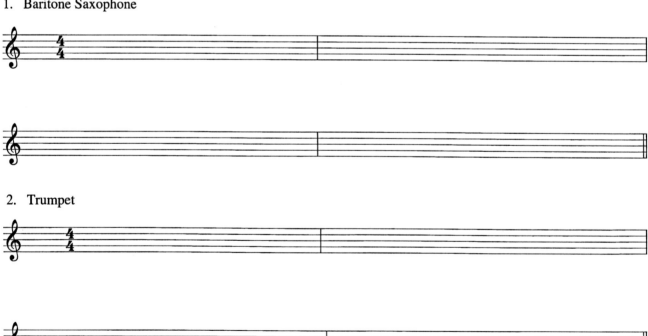

2. Trumpet

E.   Rewrite the following guitar solo for alto saxophone in the same concert key. Use the octave that allows the alto saxophone to remain in its middle register as much as possible.

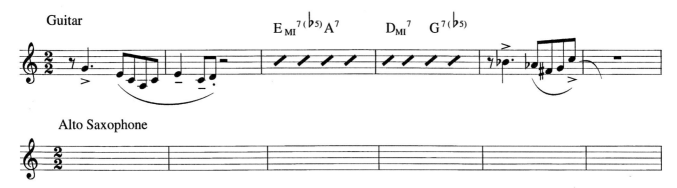

F.   Rewrite the following alto saxophone solo for tenor saxophone in the same concert key. To decide what interval to transpose the part, first find the concert key of the alto saxophone part and then transpose that key for the tenor saxophone. Once an interval of transposition is established, you can write the part using that interval throughout.

G.   The following short excerpts show a primary melody (PM) with chord symbols (a lead sheet) and the outlines of a harmonic and rhythmic support (HRS) part. You are to score these short excerpts for standard jazz ensemble using the following guidelines for each excerpt.

1.   *Bossa nova* introduction. Score the PM in octaves for the saxophones. The HRS is an upper part for the brass section background. Score this for brass, using the suggested chords. Keep the brass in good ranges by shifting from an overlapped voicing in the first two measures to a "Basie-style") close spacing (the trombones doubling the trumpets at the octave) in measures three and four. Score the rhythm parts in the standard way, indicating the style, suggesting basic rhythms, and indicating cues in the drum part for HRS rhythms that the drummer will need to know about. Devise an appropriate bass line. Edit the excerpt by supplying complete articulations and dynamics.

2.   "On Green Dolphin Street," m. 1–4. Score the PM and a close-spaced PSM texture in five parts for the saxophones. Score a HRS background in overlapped voicing for the brass. Score the rhythm parts in the standard way, indicating the style, suggesting basic rhythms, and indicating cues in the drum part for HRS rhythms that the drummer will need to know about. Devise an appropriate bass line. Edit the excerpt by supplying complete articulations and dynamics.

3.   "On Green Dolphin Street," m. 9–12. Score the PM for saxophones in octaves until the last eighth note of the second measure, which should split into harmony with a "drop 2" voicing. Score the HRS in the brass, beginning with octaves, and splitting into standard "Basie-style" close spacing (the trombones doubling the trumpets at the octave) where divisi is indicated. Score the rhythm parts in the standard way, indicating the style, suggesting basic rhythms, and indicating cues in the drum part for HRS rhythms that the drummer will need to know about. Devise an appropriate bass line. Edit the excerpt by supplying complete articulations and dynamics.

2. Kaper: "On Green Dolphin Street," m. 1–4.

3. Kaper: "On Green Dolphin Street," m. 9–12.

20   Special Considerations for Marching Band

A.   Identify each of the textural elements in the following excerpts and label, using the standard labels (PM, SM, PSM, RS, HS, HRS, SS). Review chapter 3 if you are not sure of the textural elements.

1. Hawkins, Johnson, and Dash: "Tuxedo Junction"

2. Cichy: "There is a Place, I—O—WA"

Up Tempo   ♩ =138

Arranging

3. Cichy: "Come Tuesday"

Rock

B.   Score each of the following melodies for the instrument indicated. First choose a key that will place the melody within the practical marching band range for the instrument, indicating that key in the blank below the answer staff. Now write a part for the instrument, transposing if necessary. (Refer to figure 20.19 in the text for practical ranges for marching band instruments.)

1. "Home on the Range" (cowboy song)

Flute/
Piccolo

2. "Yankee Doodle" (traditional song)

Clarinet

3. Thomas Arne: "Rule Britannia"

Alto
Saxophone

4. "Vermeland" (Swedish folk song)

Tenor
Saxophone

5. Shaker melody

Key: E♭

Trumpet

Key: __

6. William H. Glover: "In the Starlight"

Key: F

F Horn

Key: __

7. Cichy: "There is a Place, I–O–WA"

Key: F

Trombone
or
Baritone

Key: __

8. Stephen C. Foster: "Old Folks at Home"

Key: C

Tuba

Key: __

C.   Each excerpt below is a brass part (or group of parts) for marching band. Score the indicated woodwind parts, using the recommendations contained in the chapter. Notice that the brass parts are in transposed score.

1. "Home on the Range" (cowboy song)

2. John S. Smith: "The Star-Spangled Banner"

3. Samuel A. Ward: "America, the Beautiful"

4. "Auld Lang Syne" (Scotch air)

5. Samuel A. Ward: "America the Beautiful"

6. Cichy: "Cyclone Power"

7. Cichy: "Cyclone Cheer"

8. William Steffe: "Battle Hymn of the Republic"

9. Cichy: "Cyclone Power"

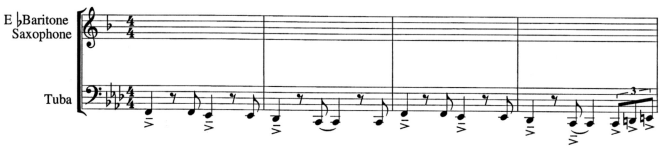

10. John S. Smith: "The Star-Spangled Banner"

D.   Set up a transposed score page with the indicated key, time signature, and style marking.

1. KEY: E♭
    TIME: 4/4
    STYLE: Swing

2. KEY: D♭
    TIME: 6/8
    STYLE: Show Biz

3. KEY: Ab
   TIME: 2/4
   STYLE: Brightly

4. KEY: F minor
   TIME: C
   STYLE: Legato

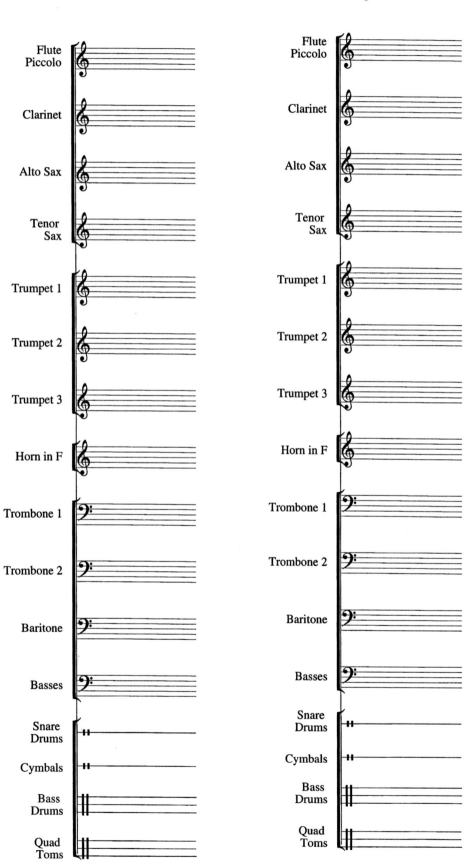

Name_____

Date _____

5. KEY: B♭
   TIME: 3/4
   STYLE: In One

6. KEY: D minor
   TIME: 4/4
   STYLE: Rock Ballad ♩ = 102

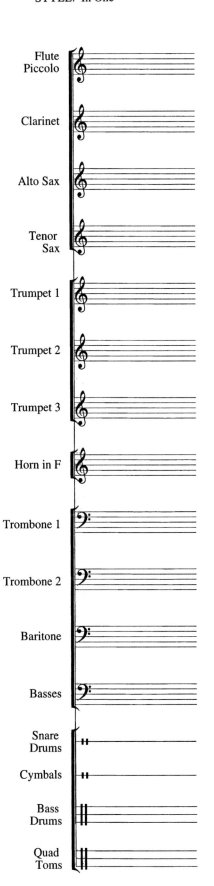
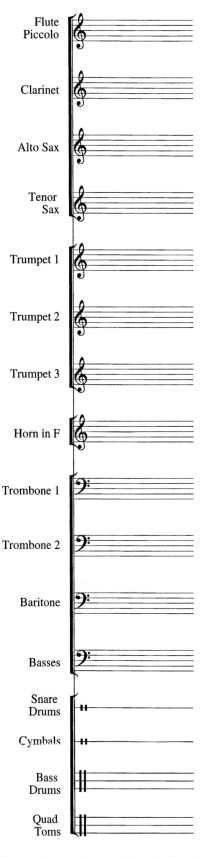

7. KEY: F
   TIME: ₵
   STYLE: March Style

8. KEY: G
   TIME: 6/8
   STYLE: Latin ♩ = 102

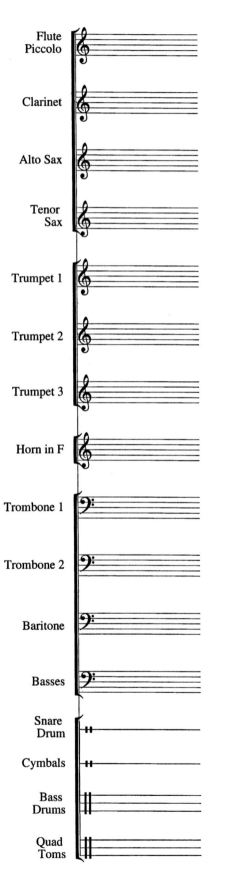

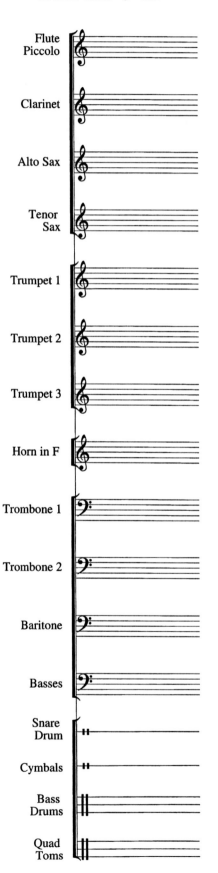

E.   Do a textural analysis and then score each of the following excerpts for marching band brass and woodwinds. Use the step-by-step method for scoring contained in the chapter.

   1. John S. Smith: "The Star-Spangled Banner"

2. Cichy: "Night Chase"

Arranging

3. Cichy: "Main Street March"

F.   Write appropriate percussion parts for each of the following excerpts, using the percussion instrumentation indicated on the score.

1. Cichy: "Cyclone Cheer"

2. Shaker melody

3. Willson: "Seventy-Six Trombones"